TOOLS FOR TEACHERS

- **ATOS:** 0.7
- **GRL:** C
- **WORD COUNT:** 29

- **CURRICULUM CONNECTIONS:** transportation

Skills to Teach

- **HIGH-FREQUENCY WORDS:** a, are, this, us
- **CONTENT WORDS:** big, car, logs, pulls, strong, takes, trailer, trash, truck(s)
- **PUNCTUATION:** exclamation point, periods
- **WORD STUDY:** long /a/, spelled *ai* (*trailer*); /k/, spelled *ck* (*trucks*)
- **TEXT TYPE:** factual description

Before Reading Activities

- Read the title and give a simple statement of the main idea.
- Have students "walk" though the book and talk about what they see in the pictures.
- Introduce new vocabulary by having students predict the first letter and locate the word in the text.
- Discuss any unfamiliar concepts that are in the text.

After Reading Activities

Trucks are strong vehicles. The book mentions different trucks that haul, pull, or move objects. Ask the children to list other kinds of trucks they know or have seen. Ask them to list other kinds of objects trucks might pull. Why do we need trucks? What kind of work do they help us do? Discuss their answers as a group.

Tadpole Books are published by Jump!, 5357 Penn Avenue South, Minneapolis, MN 55419, www.jumplibrary.com

Copyright ©2019 Jump. International copyright reserved in all countries. No part of this book may be reproduced in any form without written permission from the publisher.

Editor: Jenna Trnka **Designer:** Anna Peterson

Photo Credits: masekesam/iStock, cover; Vereshchagin Dmitry/Shutterstock, 1; Serenethos/Shutterstock, 2–3; Taina Sohlman/123rf, 4–5; lindaparton/CanStock, 6–7; Marcus Lindstrom/iStock, 8–9; Askolds/iStock, 10–11; I'm friday/Shutterstock, 12–13; Monkey Business Images/Shutterstock, 14–15.

Library of Congress Cataloging-in-Publication Data
Names: Kenan, Tessa, author.
Title: Trucks / by Tessa Kenan.
Description: Minneapolis, MN : Jump!, Inc., (2018) | Series: Let's go! | Includes index.
Identifiers: LCCN 2018002897 (print) | LCCN 2017061699 (ebook) | ISBN 9781641280020 (ebook) | ISBN 9781641280006 (hardcover : alk. paper) | ISBN 9781641280013 (pbk.)
Subjects: LCSH: Trucks—Juvenile literature. | CYAC: Trucks. | LCGFT: Picture books. | Illustrated works.
Classification: LCC TL230.15 (print) | LCC TL230.15 .K46 2018 (ebook) | DDC 629.224—dc23
LC record available at https://lccn.loc.gov/2018002897

LET'S GO!

TRUCKS

by Tessa Kenan

TABLE OF CONTENTS

tadpole books

TRUCKS

Trucks are big.

Trucks are strong.

car

This truck pulls a car.

logs

This truck pulls logs.

trailer

This truck pulls a trailer.

This truck takes trash.

This truck takes us!

WORDS TO KNOW

big

car

logs

strong

trailer

trash

INDEX

16